THE GOSPEL ACCORDING TO BOMBASTUS

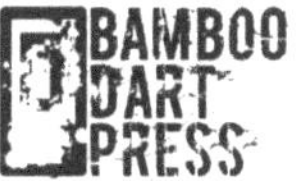

LOS ANGELES † NEW YORK † LONDON † MELBOURNE

The Gospel According to Bombastus by Brutus Chieftain & Stevo Lution

978-1-962316-19-4 Paperback
978-1-962316-20-0 Ebook

First Printing 2025

Art and design by Stevo Lution

Words by Brutus Chieftain

Editing by Kevin Ausmus

Layout by Mark Givens

For information:

Bamboo Dart Press
chapbooks@bamboodartpress.com

Bamboo Dart Press 058

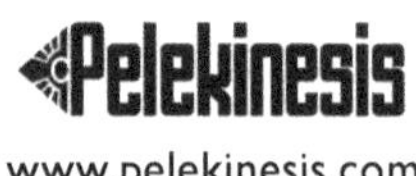

www.pelekinesis.com

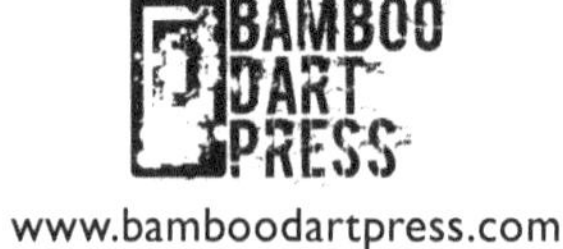

www.bamboodartpress.com

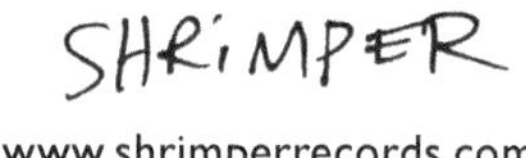

www.shrimperrecords.com

The Gospel according to BOMBASTUS

by Brutus Chieftain and Stevo Lution
edited by Kevin Ausmus

Bombastus would like to thank:
Kevin Ausmus / Mr. P
Mark Givens
Andrea and AFton Lossing
René, Jake, Michael, Kenny, and
the entire Bender Family
Doc McAdams
Michelle De Armond
Poets in Distress
The Pondwater Society
The La Brea Tar Pits

Bombastus is an artist and poet who rejects the traditional concepts of personhood, history and timelines, believing that life flows in circles, looping in and out of the circles of others - both inner and outer. For now, Bombastus believes they are an existing Neanderthal. Bombastus loved visiting the La Brea tarpits in Los Angeles as a child. Bombastus recognizes your scent. Bombastus loves you.

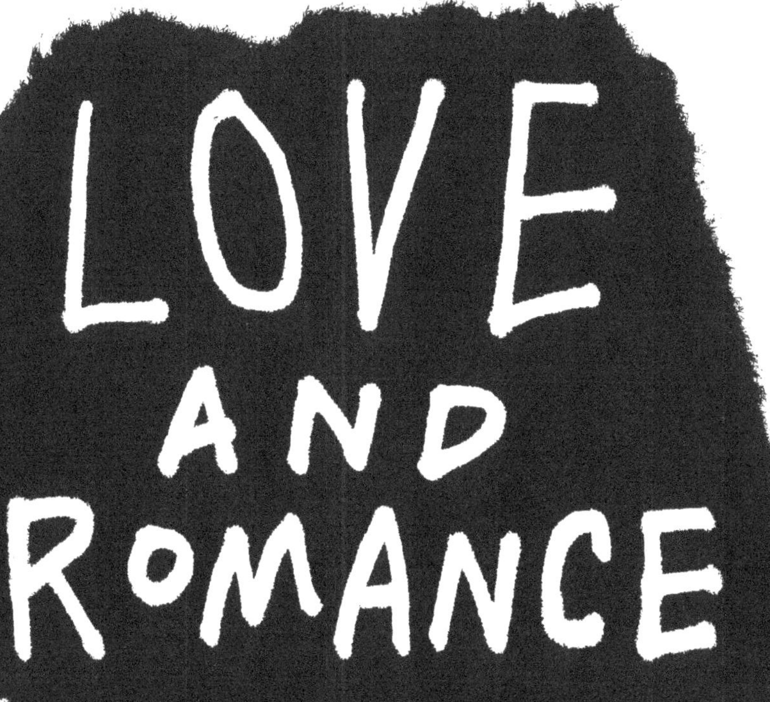
LOVE
AND
ROMANCE

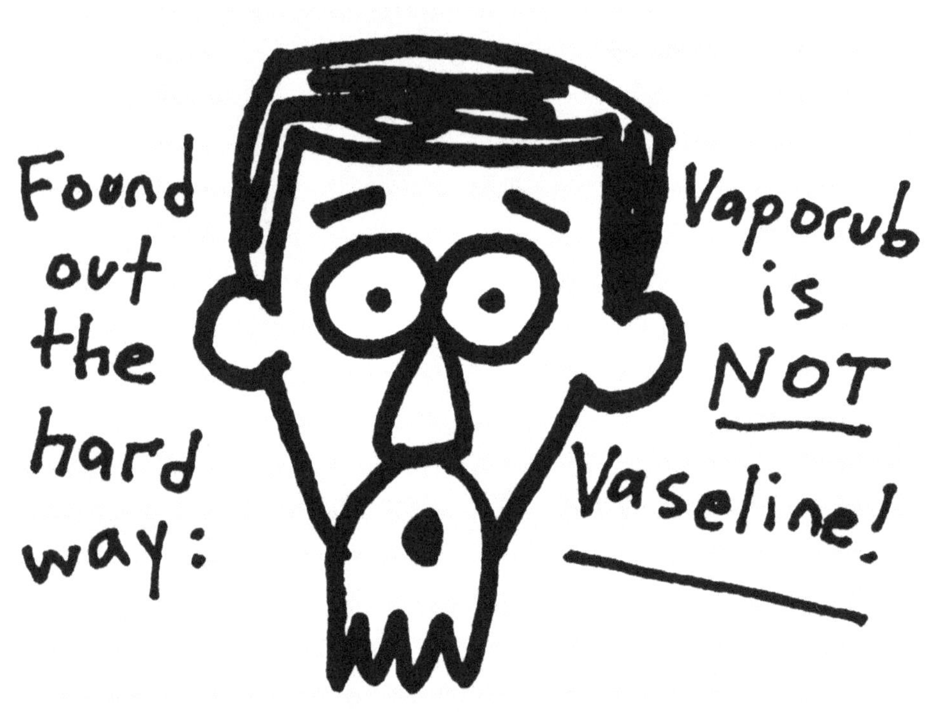
Found out the hard way:
Vaporub is NOT Vaseline!

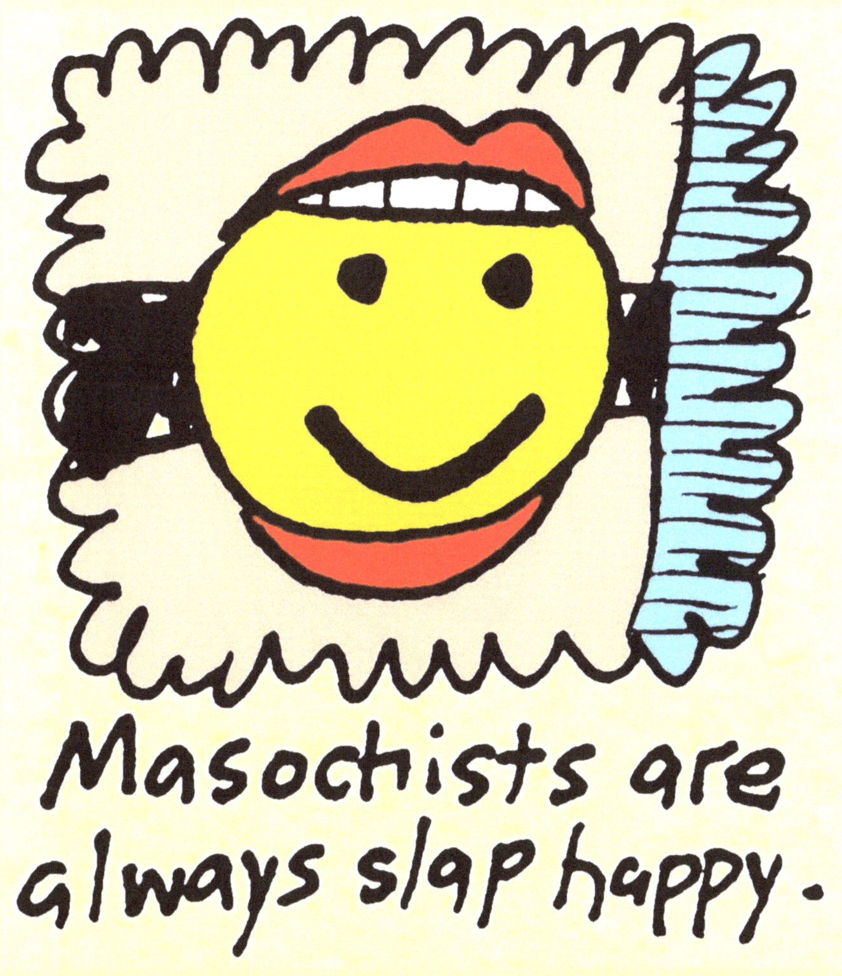
Masochists are always slap happy.

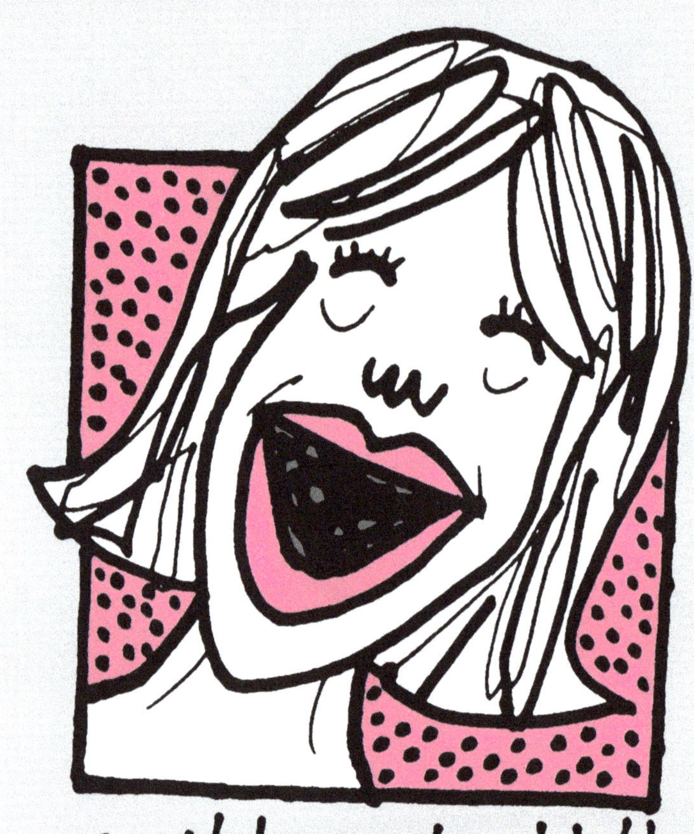

Toothless shouldn't mean loveless.

Glass-bottom boat: Lotsa Fun!

Glass-bottom honeymoon: Lotsa weird.

BIO-
LOGY

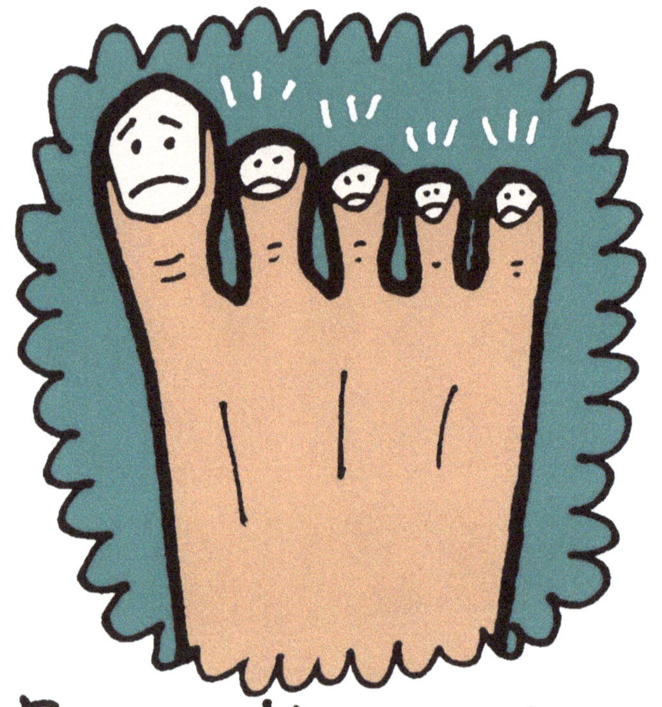

Play with your toes
once a month.
They're lonely.

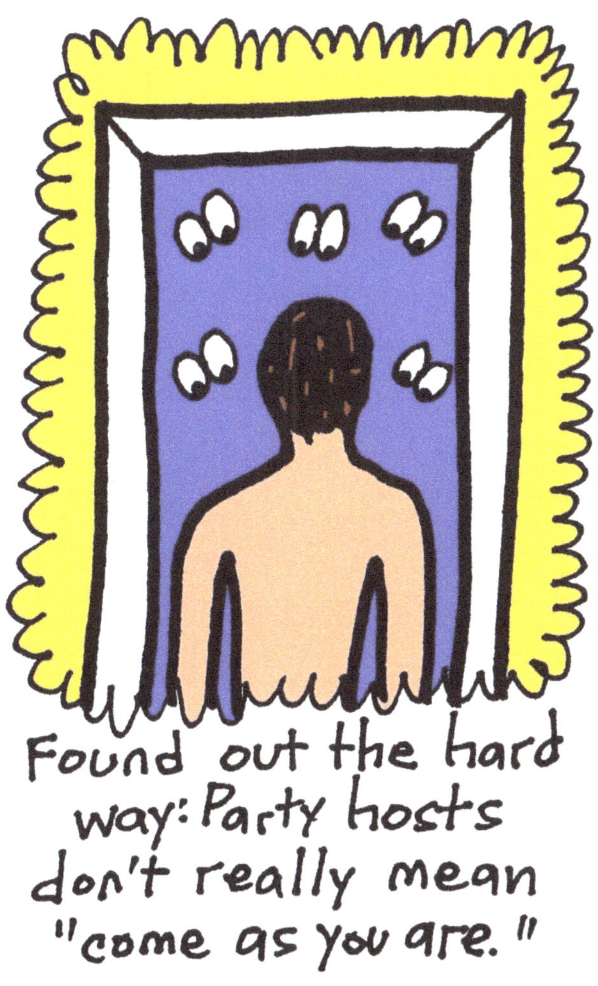
Found out the hard way: Party hosts don't really mean "come as you are."

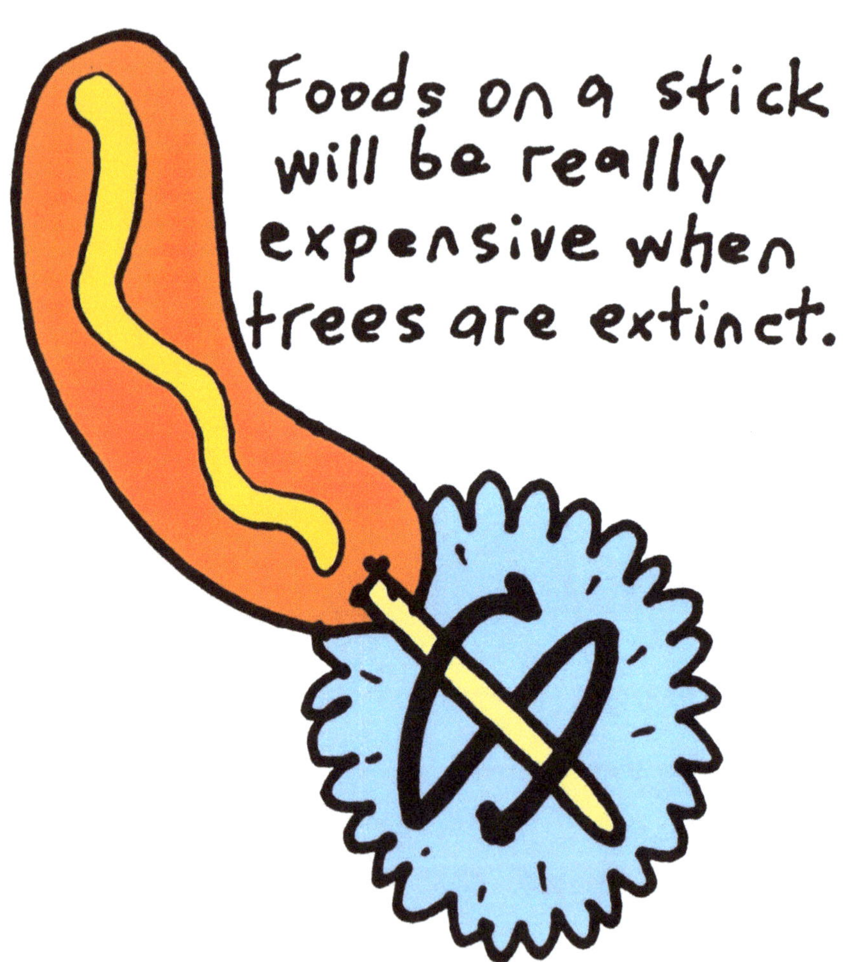
Foods on a stick
will be really
expensive when
trees are extinct.

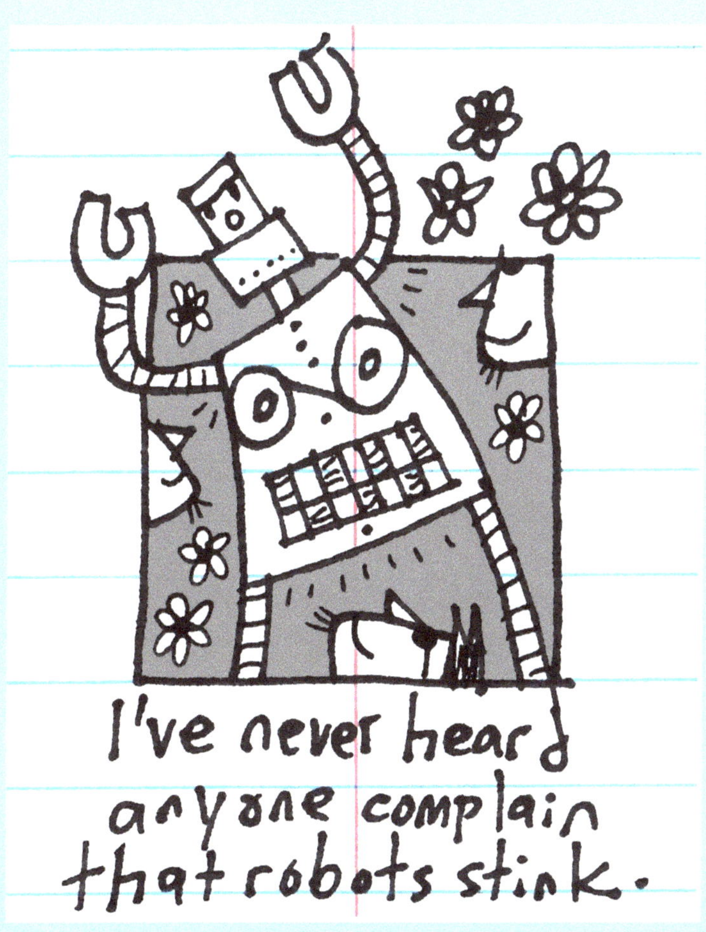
I've never heard
anyone complain
that robots stink.

PHILO-
SOPHY

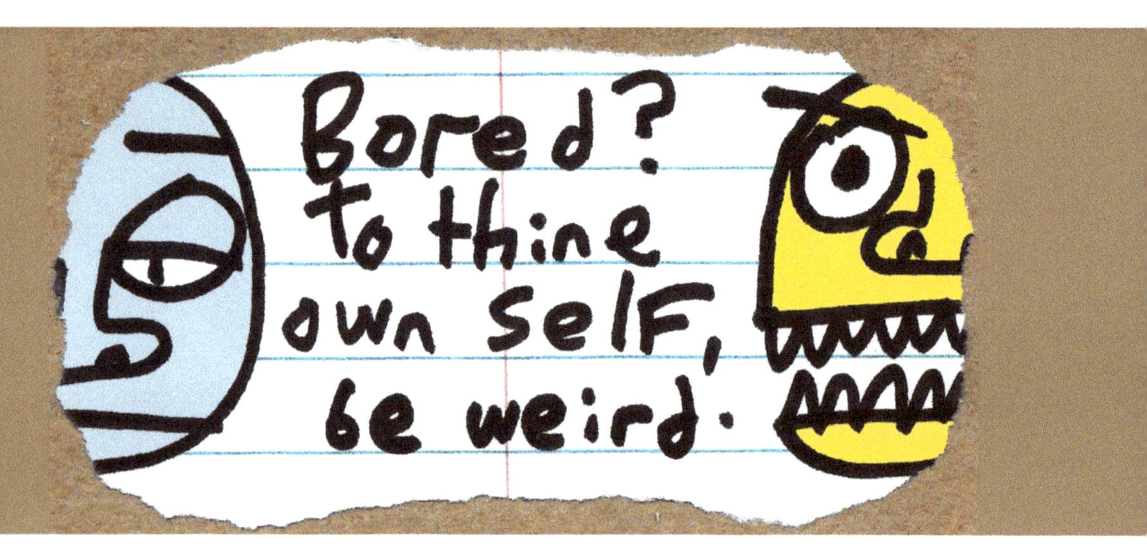
Bored?
to thine
own self,
be weird.

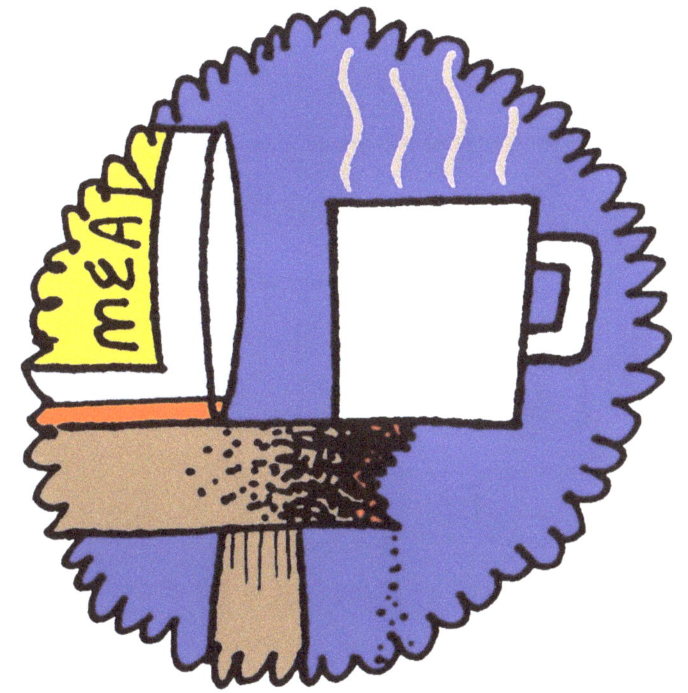

A night of fire is followed by a morning of strong coffee.

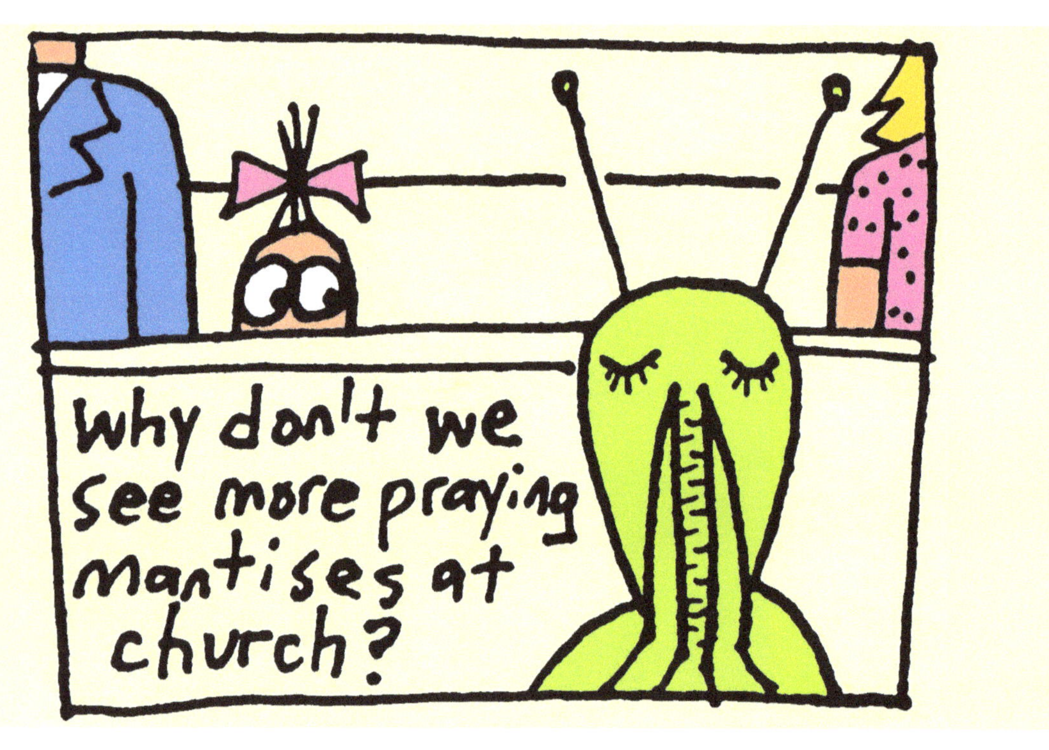
Why don't we see more praying mantises at church?

1¢
Most of the time,
"a penny for your
thoughts" is overpaying.

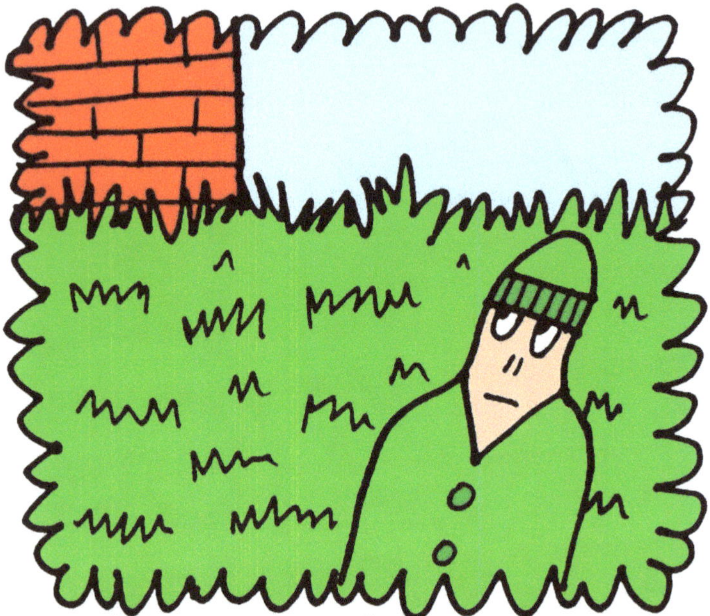

Wear only green pajamas in case you have to hide in the hedges when they come looking for you!

TRAVEL AND TOURISM

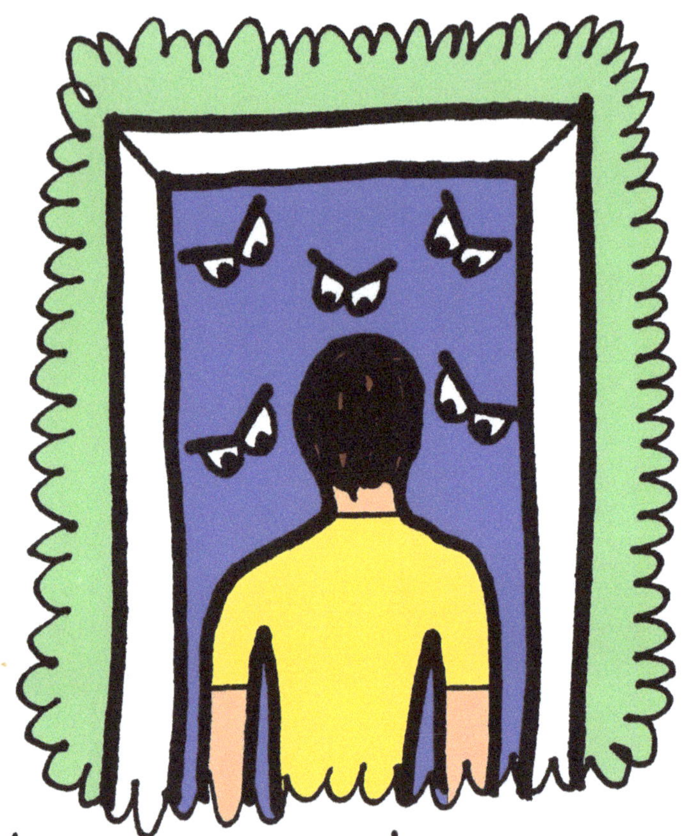

Wherever you go, there you are...
until you're asked to leave.

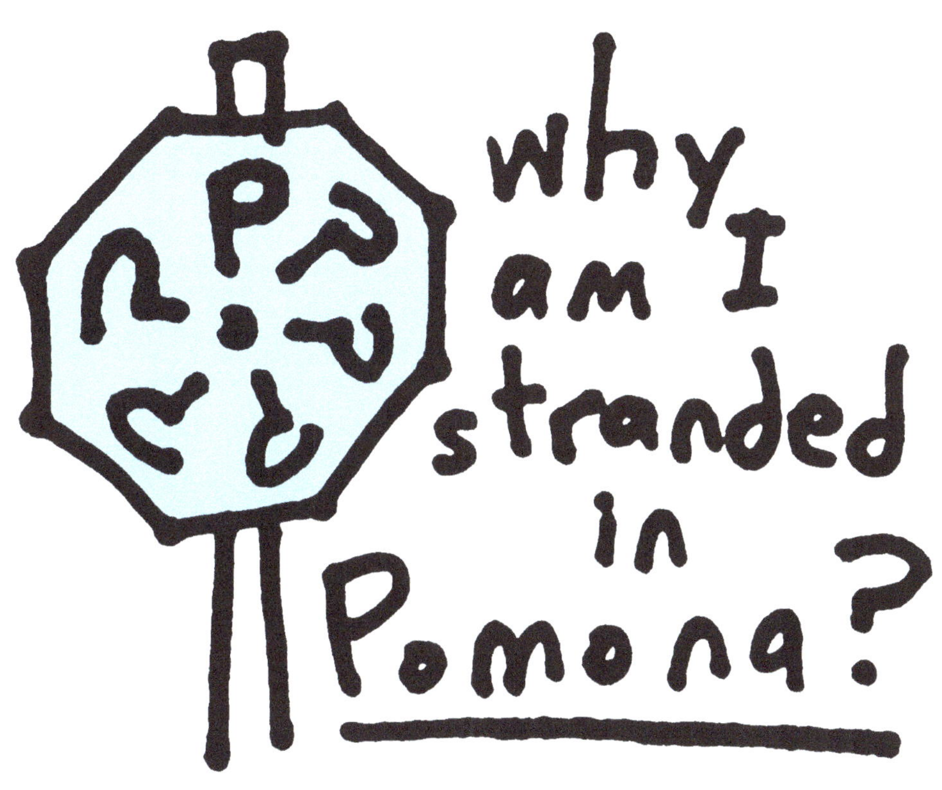
P
why
am I
stranded
in
Pomona?

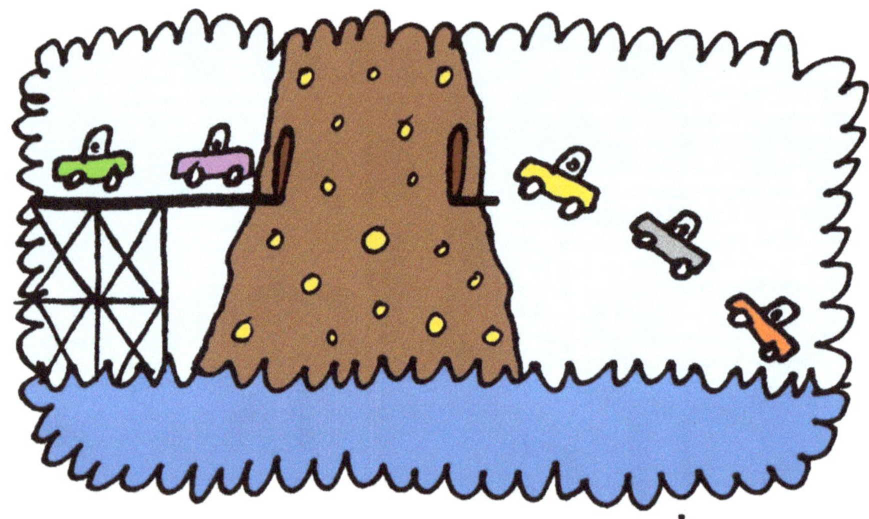

People in a hurry are going nowhere Fast.

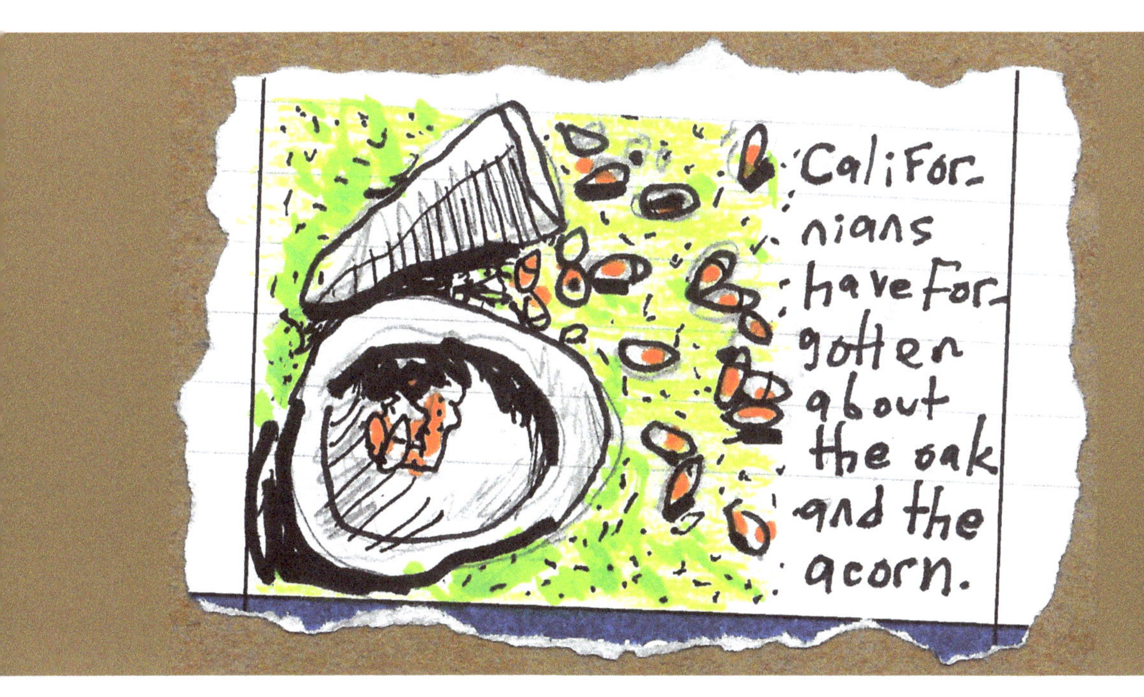
Califor-
nians
have for-
gotten
about
the oak
and the
acorn.

POLITICAL SCIENCE

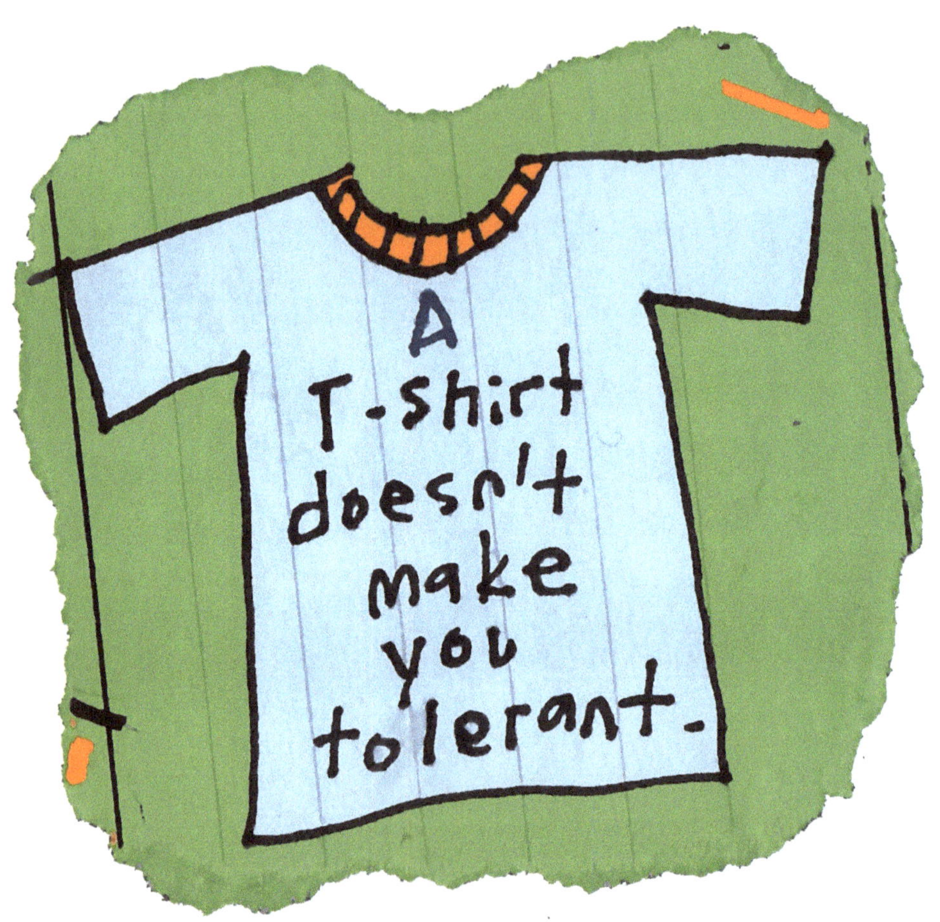
A T-shirt doesn't make you tolerant.

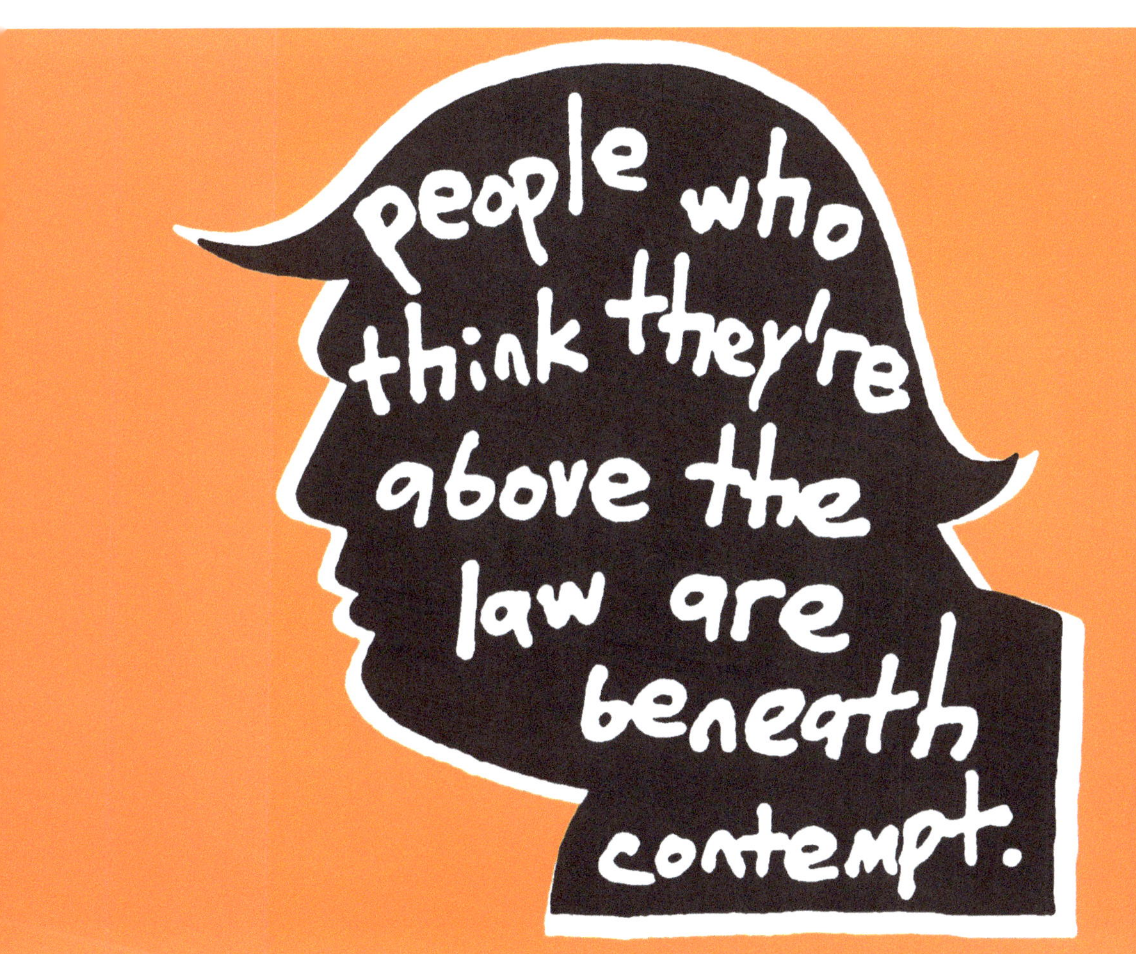
people who
think they're
above the
law are
beneath
contempt.

Scrooge was not an outlier.

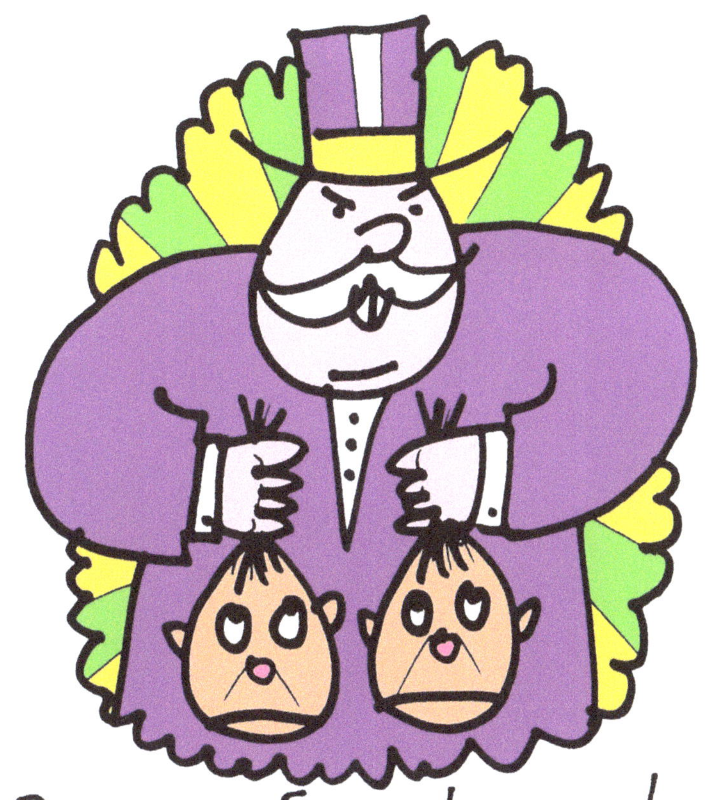

Beware of a rich man who doesn't have any Friends. He's there to take yours.

GASTRO-
NOMY

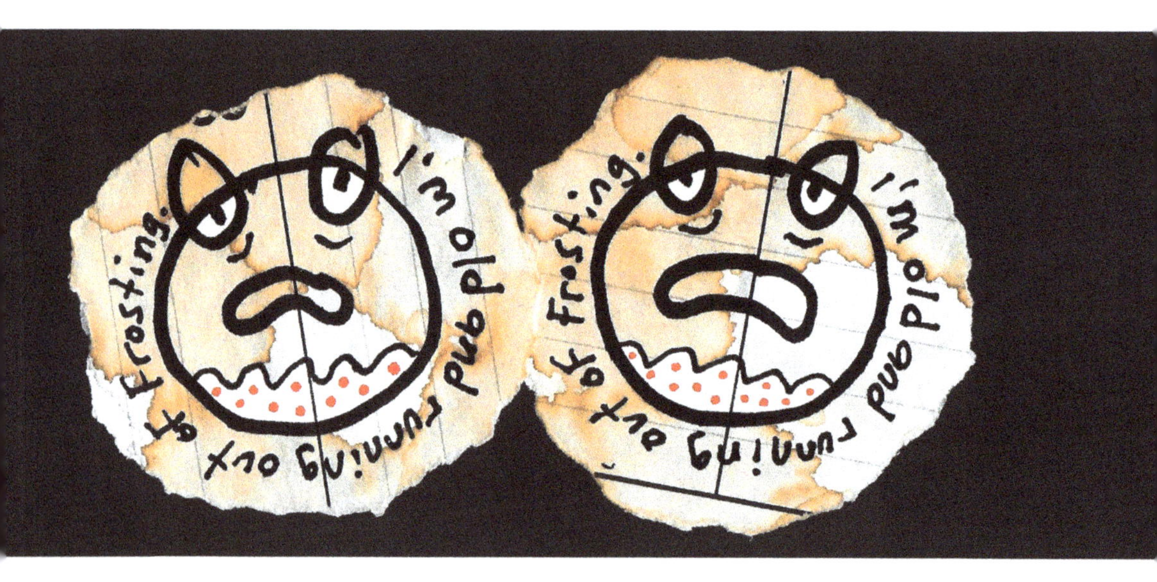
i'm old and running out of Frosting.
i'm old and running out of Frosting.

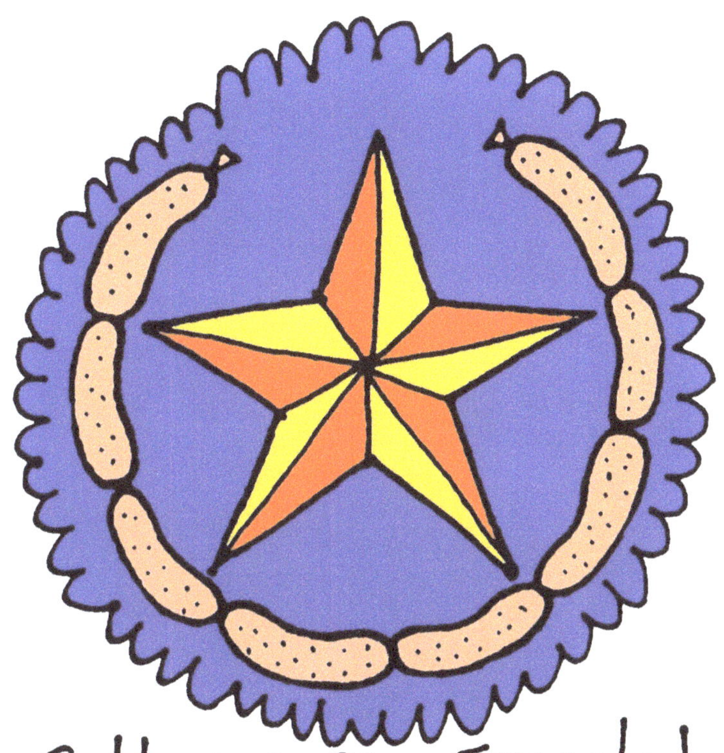

Cultures are revealed through the stuffings of their sausages.

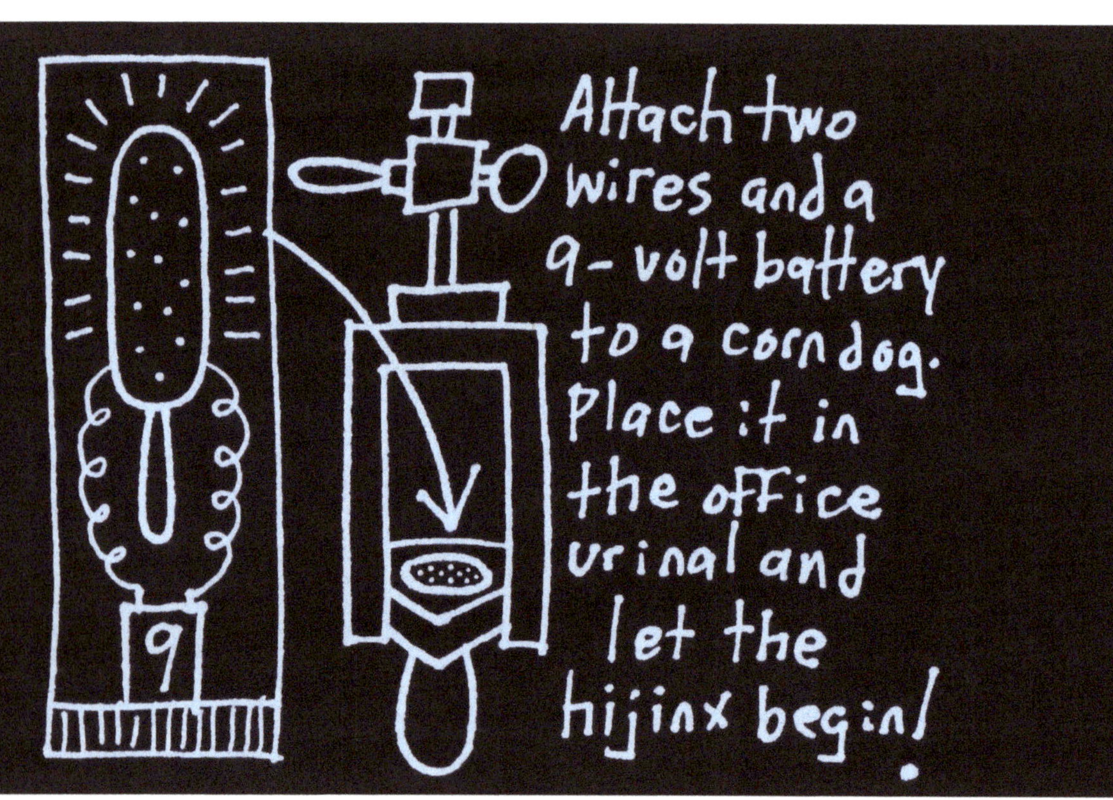
9
Attach two
wires and a
9-volt battery
to a corndog.
Place it in
the office
urinal and
let the
hijinx begin!

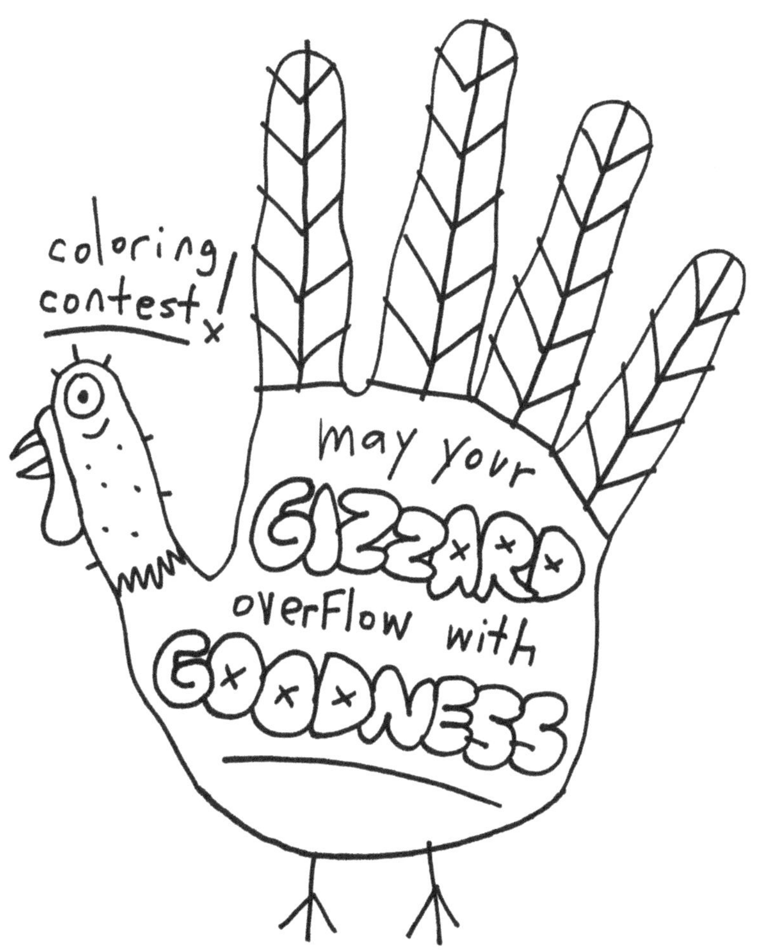
coloring contest!
may your GIZZARD overflow with GOODNESS

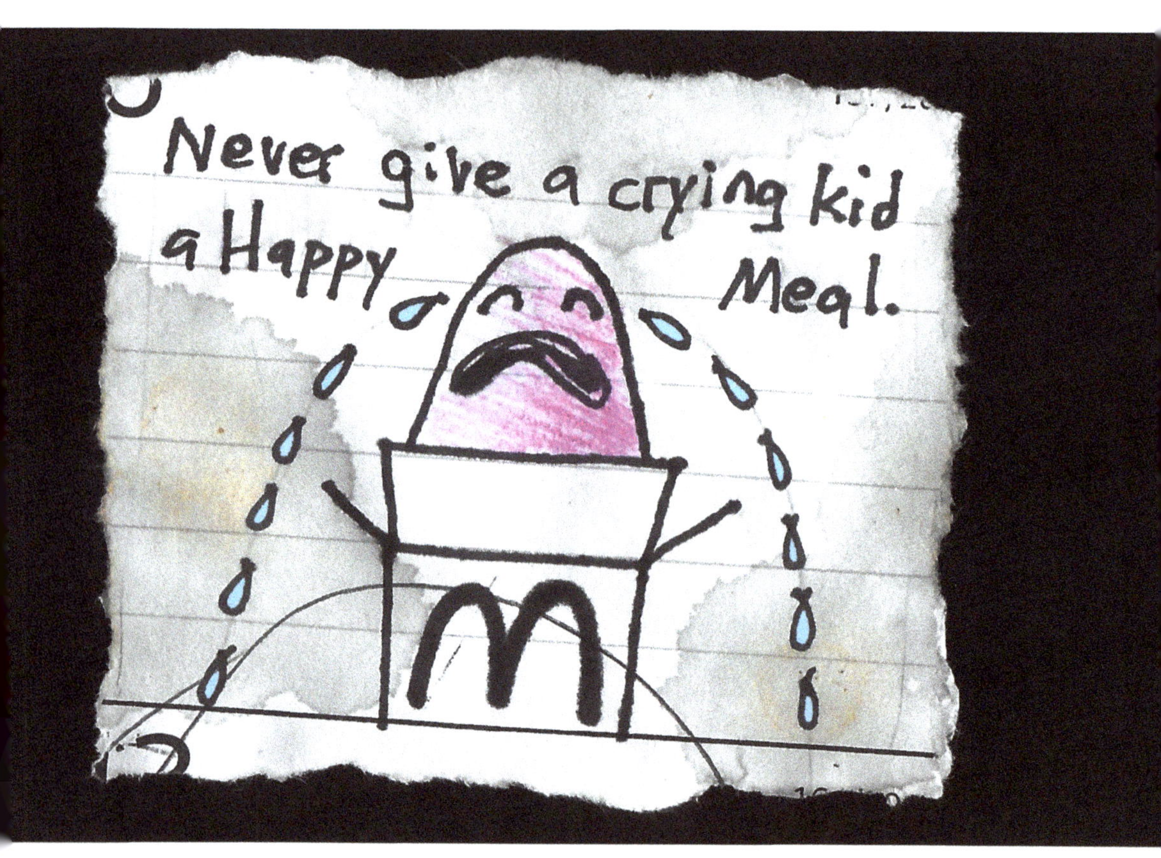
Never give a crying kid
a Happy Meal.

HEALTH AND MEDICINE

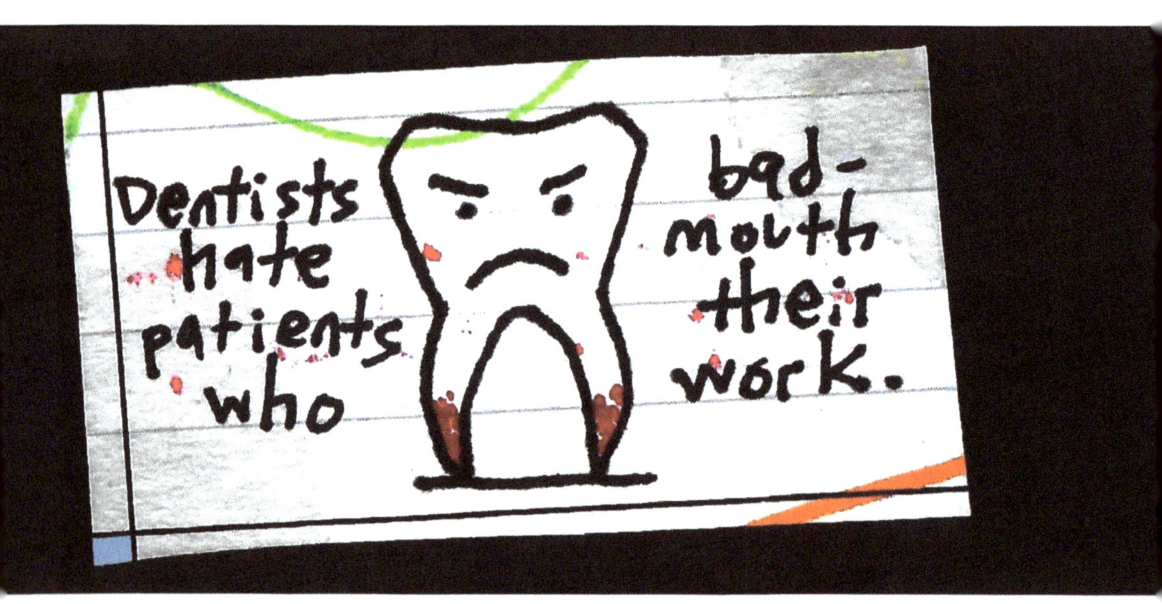
Dentists hate patients who
bad-mouth their work.

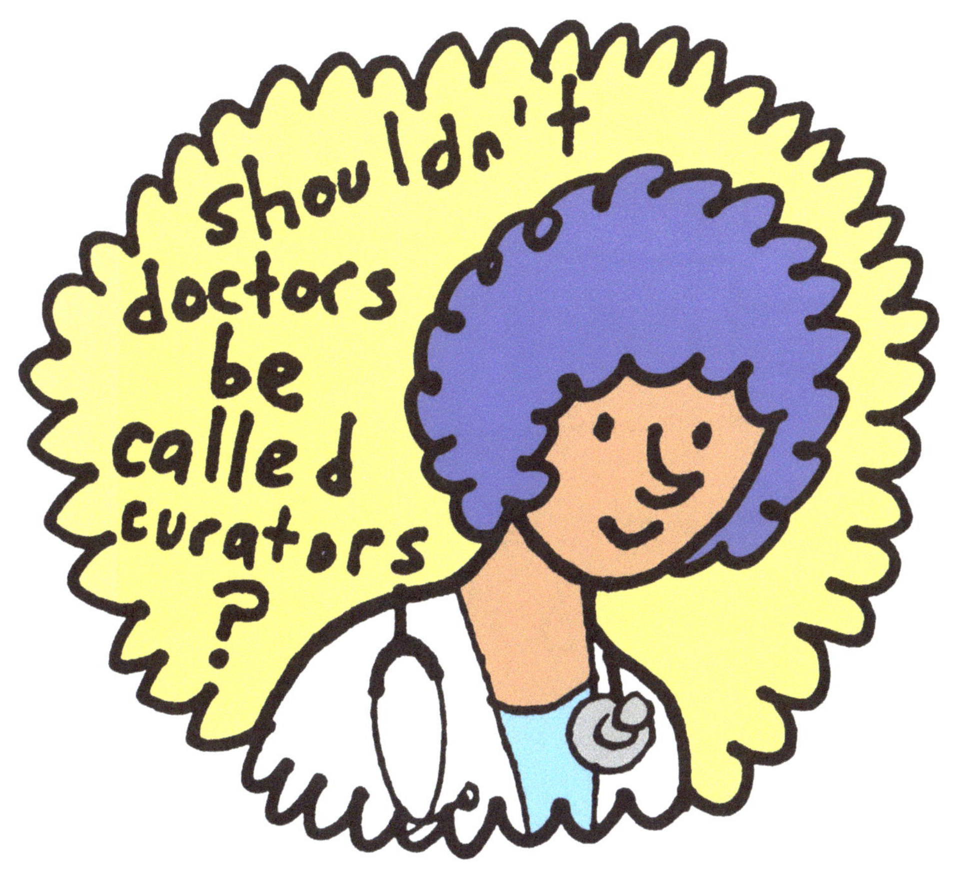
shouldn't
doctors
be
called
curators
?

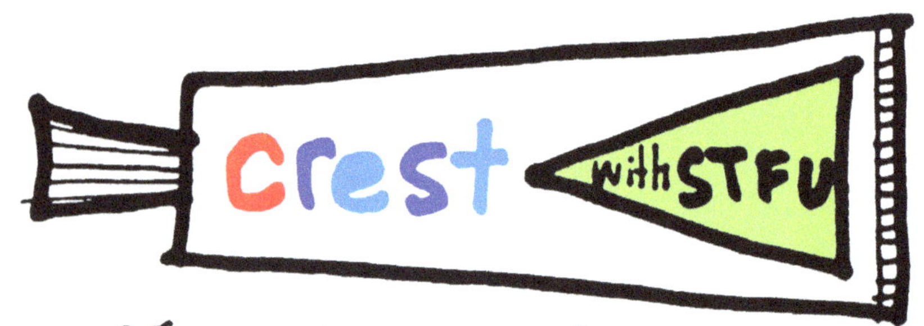

Toothpaste won't stop you from opening your big mouth.

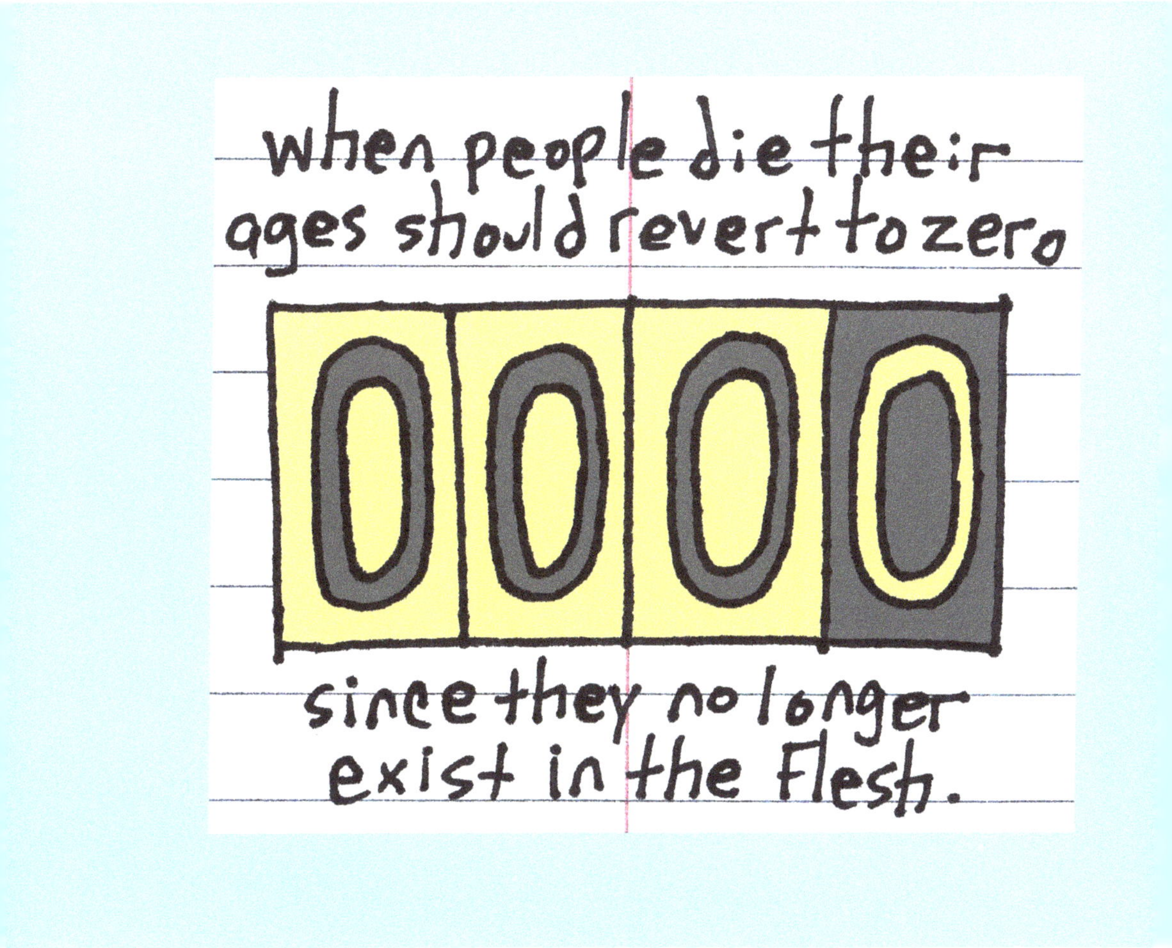

when people die their ages should revert to zero

0000

since they no longer exist in the flesh.

Bombastus is:

Poet and doghouse-bass player Johnny Bender, (AKA Brutus Chieftain), followed the Beat tradition in attitude but also enjoyed fiddling with form. He lived with his longtime wife, René, near the Box Springs Mountains in beautiful Moreno Valley. A short workshop he took with Allen Ginsberg at Naropa Institute in summer 1982 inspired Bender to start the poetry performance troupe "Poets in Distress" that same year. The group still gives raucous readings throughout Southern California. Bender also used the names Brutus Chieftain, Bombastus, Henry Heaven, Brutusaurus Rex Chieftain, Wunderbender, and John.

Born in Pomona, CA, Steve Lossing, (AKA Stevo Lution), received his first rejection notice at 16, when the high school newspaper refused to run his comic strip "Tommy the dead Trojan cat," featuring the school's deceased mascot. He received a BA in general studio art from CSUF, focusing on painting and assemblage. A long term member of performance troupe Poets in Distress, Steve currently serves as their Minister of Propaganda, drawing fliers, spray-painting signage, illustrating poetry books, designing clothing, and creating musical instruments. His political art can be spotted throughout the Inland Empire on light poles, signposts, and Jane Wiedlin's guitar at Coachella. Steve lives in Riverside, CA with his wife Andrea, their daughter, Afton, Prince Shiny the chug, and countless feral cats.

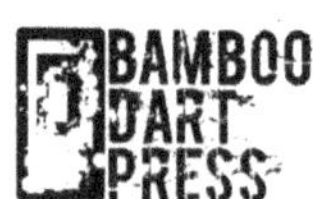

112 N. Harvard Ave. #65

Claremont, CA 91711

chapbooks@bamboodartpress.com

www.bamboodartpress.com

www.ingramcontent.com/pod-product-compliance
Lightning Source LLC
Chambersburg PA
CBHW042052030726
47599CB00019B/2457
9781962316194